Voices of Vets

Voices of Vets

A Bridge Back to the World

Poems from veterans and their families

GREENFIRE PRESS

GreenFire Press
An Imprint of Mosaic Multicultural Foundation

Contents

FOREWORD

A TERRIBLE BEAUTY IS BORN

The soul searching words of wonder and power that make up the poems in this book were distilled from the lived experiences of a group of war veterans and their family members who attended a five-day retreat in May 2008. Their words were shaped during the heart-felt retreat and presented on the stage of the Angus Bowmer Theatre at the Oregon Shakespeare Festival on Memorial Day.

To paraphrase Jane Austen, "It was not good theatre; it was the best." It was compelling work, born of courage and blood, heat and memory. The voices of the veterans blazed through the theater with a rare authority and a devastating beauty—stunning the hearts of the audience and offering an unforgettable experience of anguish and awe that still reverberates throughout the town.

How did it happen that a small town in Oregon opened its heart and provided a healing welcome to veterans of recent wars? While traveling in Ireland, filmmaker Kim Shelton had a vision of creating a welcome home event for veterans of the wars in Iraq and Afghanistan. The idea involved honoring veterans for their service and making a documentary film that might inspire others to create welcoming events.

Once back in Ashland, Oregon, Kim and her husband, therapist Bill McMillan began gathering support from individuals, organizations and businesses. In addition to winning local support, Kim and Bill visited Veterans Centers and spoke with vets, counselors, therapists, and advisors. After much discussion, three experts in working with trauma joined the staff of the event. When combined, Mike Maxwell, Carl Robinson, and Lauren McLagen brought over fifty years of experience counseling and working with battle veterans and personal traumas.

Knowing that someone would have to provide the imagination and leadership necessary for healing, Kim and Bill invited Michael Meade and Jacob Lakatua of the Mosaic Multicultural Foundation. Meade is a singular human being who not only creates ceremonies of deep healing, but also inspires high creativity in others. He knows, from rare personal experience, that it is possible to enter places of unimaginable suffering and generate art through speaking the truth found in human anguish, sorrow, despair, rage, and pain. He also knows the importance of having that art witnessed by others.

Michael has worked the alchemy of art and healing with many people, including prisoners, gang youth, refugees, and veterans. He calls the resulting language "immediate poetry." This book offers a collection of such immediate, soulful speaking and writing.

The retreat period was filled with ceremonial cleansing, storytelling, singing, remembering, reading poetry, and "getting poetry and truth into the room." This "community of imagination and memory" was forged through weeping and raging, through speaking out and writing things down. We, the witnesses, knew we were being poured into a cauldron of creation, where the realities of surviving a war were being distilled into a truth that could either kill or cure. And the only way out was to go all the way through as the intensities of war and tragedy bled into the room.

The veterans and family members are the most courageous people I have ever known; men and women willing to confront their wounds directly and openly. "I am a shell of who I was." "Most of me is still in Iraq." "I just wanted to bring my guys home to their moms." "Be my mom, bring me home." "Nobody told us how to heal the soul."

Yet they found in the room many paths to healing the soul as they spoke of the terrible vulnerability of battle wounds and Post Traumatic Stress Disorders. Out beyond the heartbreak and loss, the wounding and sorrows, the traumatic stress of many years' duration, these amazing men and women created a community of authentic and enduring mutual support and caring. From the essence of their experiences in and around war, they created a unique and pulsing work of art. They stood on a stage in a theatre —itself a temple to the invincibility of the human spirit—and spoke these words, sang these songs, to an enraptured, awestruck, totally welcoming audience.

From the gathered wounds and shared courage a terrible beauty has been born. It can sear the heart, yet it can also bring a healing touch to those willing to welcome and embrace our veterans and their lived stories.

PEGGY RUBIN

INTRODUCTION

WAR, THE UNDERWORLD, AND INITIATION

The experience of war alters a person's way of being in the world. Even those who come through battles physically unscathed are forever changed within themselves. In war conditions a certain courage must be found within as both life and death must be faced. Afterwards, nothing in the world or in oneself can ever be quite the same again. Those who survive the gravities of war carry a darker knowledge of the world and of the human heart.

Initiation is an old name for any process that changes a person completely. What begins as a simple choice, a sudden impulse, or the need to answer a call becomes an adventure that changes a person forever. The initiate enters this territory of change as a novice and rises through the ranks by virtue of suffering dangers and surviving trying circumstances. Those who survive "earn their stripes" and become an "old hand" or "veteran."

In old tribal groups the stripes that indicated rank were actual scars made in the arm itself in order to indicate that certain experiences leave an indelible mark on a person. Typically, experiences of war leave a person with scars and stripes, with physical marks and wounds, as well as recurring memories and traumatic images that penetrate and lacerate the soul.

War presents a particular kind of "underworld initiation"

in which life turns upside-down and death becomes a constant presence - a dark revelation waiting behind each boulder, bunker, and bush. As life's surface layers are stripped away soldiers and warriors enter not just a foreign territory, but an explosive "otherworld" where a darker knowledge prevails, where the intensities and horrors of battle can alter the mind and the heart in ways that seem irreparable.

Upon returning from the battlefields where life fights with death - where loyalty and care are fully tested - battle veterans can find the civilian world superficial and daily life tame and unaware. Unless the inner initiatory process can be brought to a conclusion that matches the intensity of battle, the common world can remain awkwardly foreign and coldly unwelcoming for those who try to return from the underworld of war.

The human psyche tends to experience life-altering adventures in a three-step pattern: separation, ordeal, and return. Typically, life-changing experiences begin with a departure that leaves the daily world far behind—a felt separation that leads a person away from family and friends and into unknown and threatening territories. There may be a new group or cadre to join, but there is also an experience of being completely separate and alone in foreign circumstances. The felt sense of separation sets the scene for the psyche to experience the world anew and to respond to life in ways that may have seemed impossible just moments before.

The second step of initiation involves ordeals and suffering. A person earns their stripes by facing specific challenges, by learning new things, by struggling to develop, fit in and measure up, by surviving whatever difficulties and dangers might appear. Since each person is a unique and specific arrangement of qualities and limitations, each has a specific breaking point as well as untapped potentials. What comes easily to one can be a huge struggle for another; what intrigues or excites one person can terrify or traumatize another. The circumstances of war and battle may be shared by the whole squad, but the experiences will affect each member differently and mark them uniquely.

The intensity of battle brings out the most terrifying aspects of humanity as well as deeply courageous and altruistic qualities.

Heroic qualities and callous disregard for life can erupt in the same person—self-sacrificing courage and paralyzing fear can exchange places moment to moment. During life-changing events it is the exact nature of the individual psyche that determines which experiences become defining or defeating, damning or redeeming. It is the specific lived story that takes shape inside each soldier that becomes both the tale of trauma and the potential source of healing.

For those who remain in the altered state triggered by battle, the daily world seems unaware, overly calm, and sharply ignorant of the sudden intensities and penetrating tragedies of life. Not only is daily life dull by comparison, but the immediacy, loyalty and radical closeness of companions is missing. Despite the palpable possibilities of death and dismemberment, many soldiers prefer to return to the battlefield in order to continue the close bonds of loyalty and unspoken understanding of battle comrades.

Any meaningful return and recovery from the life-threatening, life-damaging, and life-altering experiences of battle will also involve the specific details and precise qualities of the individual. Induction into service may occur as a group, but those who are able to integrate their experiences in healthy ways will each do so differently. Thus, the unique story of each veteran becomes the essential ground for recovery, the language for healing, and the path towards re-integration to the community in meaningful ways.

Whether a war is deemed successful or disastrous, the effects of battle continue to rage inside the warriors in wounds that torture the body and shocks that continue to trouble the soul. The recurring demons of battle involve terrifying visions of exploding body parts, haunting memories of slain friends, even the biting presence of guilt for having survived the death-ridden roads of hell. Like most traumas the effects of battle are not limited to those who experienced them directly. The unresolved traumas of battle rattle the sleep of entire families and post-traumatic stresses readily become inherited forms of anxiety. The terrors and traumas of war don't simply disappear but become a troubled inheritance for an entire society.

The third step of an initiatory process involves a reinstatement within one's community. Battle wounds suffered in service of a community also require community involvement for genuine healing. It may be the government that calls people to battle, but it is the families and communities of the warriors that must welcome and receive them back - that must help them to heal both the visible and invisible wounds and make them whole members of society again. A genuine return from the battlefield requires an acknowledgment of the warriors' sacrifices as well as genuine healing of the wounds to both their bodies and their souls—a conscious recognition of what each individual has suffered and a genuine acknowledgement of how they have been altered and changed. The third step involves both taking the war out of the warrior and returning the veteran to a meaningful and respected place in the common community.

When the third step is omitted or handled in a superficial way the entire process remains unfinished and a strong tendency to repeat the first two steps over and over will remain. Instead of healing and healthy integration a repetition syndrome develops exactly where the traumatic aspects and overwhelming ordeals mark the individual psyche. Feelings of being alien to one's own family and community grow unless such feelings become integrated in a revisioned sense of life. It is not just that veterans have experienced things that their friends and families don't understand, but also that their own psyches remain caught in a betwixt and between condition and an unresolved state. Many veterans become literally homeless - abandoned in and by their own communities after sacrificing parts of their bodies and souls for their homeland.

Post-traumatic stress syndrome (PTSD) can also be described as being stuck in an unfinished initiation where the ordeal stage continues in the form of overwhelming and unresolved memories, emotions, anxieties, and conflicts. If a meaningful return does not occur, the demons of war continue to tear at the fabric of the individual souls and at the life of the community. When considered from the view of life-changing initiations the traumatic conditions are not simply an issue for the individual involved, but also for the community that fostered the intense encounters with life and death. Although initiatory events begin with a separation and even isolation of the individual, they cannot properly conclude unless a conscious and caring community becomes involved.

The suffering and sacrifice of veterans must be acknowledged at a genuine human level just as quality medical treatments must reflect the nature of physical wounds. Just as the service of the warrior is intended to transcend personal needs and fears, the return of the veterans requires something greater and deeper than life as usual on the part of their communities. A genuine rite of return involves an open and compassionate community that fully acknowledges the courage and the wounds of those who return from battle as well as fully grieves those whose lives ended in the unforgiving fields of war.

Voices of Vets represents one of many efforts to welcome veterans back from the tragedies and calamities of war. This process involves an intentional revival and retelling of the traumatic experiences and troubling memories engendered by the circumstances of war. Not just the sharing of "war stories," but an emotional return to the most traumatic events in order to give full expression to them and shape them into artful forms that can help hold and heal them. It also requires the presence of a community willing to listen with compassion and understanding as the psychic wounds are reopened and the losses are recounted, honored and respected.

Voices of Vets recreates the three-step process of initiation in non battle circumstances. First, the veterans separate from daily life again and prepare to face the emotional and psychological conditions that surround their war experiences. Physical, emotional, and even spiritual conditions awaken in such a gathering and can be consciously faced again.

Giving full expression to traumatic experiences becomes the second step of the Voices process and the new ordeal through which still raw events and traumatic patterns can become vehicles of understanding and healing. Fellow veterans serve as the first witnesses and instinctive community that openly accepts the story of each participant. The camaraderie experienced in battle conditions becomes rekindled as veterans witness each other's stories and support each other's efforts to capture the emotions and memories in specific language. Although the whole story may never be told, life threatening moments and enduring feelings become the raw material for a kind of "immediate poetry" that helps to reshape the radical experiences and reveal the essence of each story as well as the courage and value of each person.

In the surprising openness generated by the deep sharing of individual stories and the renewed sense of camaraderie that develops, a range of healing experiences can occur.

In a kind of "post battle triage" people instinctively help to heal each other and spontaneous mentoring develops, especially between older and younger veterans. The instinctive camaraderie of war veterans offers a natural resource for genuine healing, a basis for enduring relationships and a context for finding individual life purpose.

The final step in this process—and the only proper conclusion—involves a respectful public gathering in which the community at large can witness the stories and learn the concerns of its veterans. Such an event is different from a typical Veterans' Day and is intended to reach a deeper place than simple patriotism or personal politics. Since it is the humanity of a person that sacrifices and suffers during war, it is the deep humanity in a person that must be acknowledged, welcomed back, and consciously celebrated.

Governments bear heavy responsibilities to those it sends to war and to their families and community members should insist that those responsibilities are fulfilled. Yet, even if public agencies did their job, the work of the community begins where the official duties end. Only an attentive, compassionate and engaged community can accept the veterans as they actually are upon return, with wounds and scars, with penetrating memories and traumas, with nightmares and flashbacks and confounding confusions. The role of the community is to witness compassionately -to accept those returning on their own terms as the living voices of the tragedy and nobility of human life. Genuine public ceremonies can provide healing for all involved and opportunities for greater understanding of the effects of both public policies and of the private tragedies visited upon the human soul.

At the Buckhorn Springs retreat, family members joined the veterans and offered their own experiences of loss and wounding as well as their astute knowledge of "second-hand PTSD." The presence of spouses and family members reflected the actuality of life after combat and ardently revealed how the effects of war extend far beyond those who actually enter the battlefields. As demonstrated in the poetry and stories that follow, the retreat setting allows painful stories to be told and individual suffering to be exposed in ways that add to a deeper understanding for each family as well as a greater healing for each veteran. It's not that each veteran must have family members present, rather that some family being present makes "family" a presence for all involved. War can suddenly become an "out of body experience;" it also can become an experience of "loss of soul." Some wounds to the soul cause parts of a person to feel exiled from their own humanity and only cease to ache and anguish a person after they have been fully welcomed back into the nobility and caring heart of the human family.

A poet once said that this world is not made of atoms- it is made of stories. The world never seems to run out of conflicts or of war stories; yet this world is also made of healing stories and little tales of redemption. In order to bring out the essential stories of those trying to return from battle it helps to begin with a mythic tale that offers a framework and opens the territories of ordeal and survival. We began the Buckhorn Springs retreat with an African story that depicts a visit to the underworld where both traumatic wounding and golden qualities become revealed.

Maggots and Gold begins with a brother and sister walking across a wide field in the bright light of day. Suddenly, their father appears before them and gestures for them to follow him. They are greatly surprised to see their father because he had died some time before. The father leads the sister and brother to an opening in the ground that becomes a road that leads to a village under the world.

Once in the underworld village the children are instructed to hide in some bushes and observe what happens. As they watch a crowd comes followed by a royal person who turns to reveal one side of his body to be rotting flesh covered with maggots. The crowd of people cleans the rotting flesh and removes the maggots. The next day the scene repeats except that the royal person turns the other side to the crowd. The second side turns out to be golden and the crowd proceeds to anoint it with oil and polish it until it shines.

On the third day the father returns and asks for a report. The brother and sister confide that the first day revealed maggots and the second day gold. The father tells them that they will have bad luck in life and will follow roads of grief and hardship because they saw the rotting flesh and maggots first. Had they come on a different day their lives would be blessed and their road easier and less tormented. He then leads the sister and brother back up to the place where the underworld opens back to the world above. The brother and sister re-enter the common field of life and continue on their way with much to deliberate and discuss about what they saw in the underworld and what lies before them on the roads of life.

The veterans picked up the tale and expanded it by inserting their own experiences of the underworld of war with its rotting flesh and its surprising revelations of golden qualities amidst the carnage. Their literal battle experiences fleshed out the story's metaphors and their emotions brought the tale to life. It turned out that many had seen and even handled rotting flesh; that they remained haunted by those experiences. Everyone had seen horrors of some kind - each had a maggot tale and a need to tell it. Many expressed feelings of being betrayed by authority figures both during the battles and in the diagnoses and prognoses that followed their return from war's underworld.

Yet, each could also describe moments when the gold of human caring and love shone through the red fog of war and the dense and frustrating atmosphere of war's aftermath. The loyalty and courage of friends, the love and care of family members, the surprise occasions of beauty and healing needed to be spoken out and polished by a community paying real attention and helping to bring light to the darkest parts of the soul.

The cleaning of the rotten flesh and polishing of the hidden gold began in the relative safety of the veterans' retreat, but could only be finished in the midst of the village of common community that required the original sacrifices in the first place. At the public gathering, the old mythic tale was told and enriched with the abundant addition of the painful and beautiful stories of the veterans and their families. Amidst the shared pain and anguish some gold began to shine through and the best qualities of life could be seen and felt and anointed again as our shared humanity polished up everyone in attendance.

The poems that follow here are the direct expression of the courage of returning veterans and their families. They represent stories that too often go untold, feelings that too often remain unexpressed, and realities that too easily become ignored in the aftermaths of war. The voices of veterans offer the anguished speech of war, but also express the essential human desire for healing and for meaning to be found even in the most tragic experiences of life. As one of the veterans asks us all in a poem: "Can we create a village as strong as a war?"

MICHAEL MEADE

I

Maggots and Gold

I DON'T KNOW

Katrina's 5. Mom's 25. Mom's going to war—soon, too soon, not soon enough. I don't know. We are watching, "We Were Soldiers." She says, "Mommy, that's war." "Oh, Sweety, don't worry, Momma's just driving trucks."

January 15th, no sleep. Making love to him for the last time —maybe—could be—maybe not—I don't know. Kisses. So many kisses, tears, I love you's. I miss you right now! I'm not even gone and I miss you right now! Don't let go of me. I can't get close enough. Tighter.

I turned off the alarm. Who needs it. It's January 16th, 4:00AM. I am in the shower with him. He brushes my hair. I put it up according to military regulation. Brown T-shirt, DCU bottoms, tuck in, chinch the belt, wool socks, tan boots. DCU top. IDENTIFICATION TAGS! For just in case. Maybe, could be—maybe not—I don't know.

How does a mother say goodbye to her five year old child? What kind of goodbye is it? Is it the last goodbye? Maybe, could be, maybe not—I don't know. So kiss her while she sleeps, pat her strawberry blond hair, one last take-it-all-in glance. Turn around—don't look back—keep going and walk out the door. For the last time? Maybe—could be —maybe not— I don't know.

MANDY MARTIN
U.S. ARMY, IRAQ VETERAN

NO WORDS

She couldn't say don't go
   There were no words
She watched as the bags were packed

She listened quietly, didn't make a fuss
   There were no words
Phones rang, quiet conversations

Pictures were drawn with Dad's big gun
   There were no words
Neighbors came with good wishes

Voices were kept hushed, but everybody knew
   There were no words
More bags were packed and now we knew the day

Last kiss, last hug, "Be good, I love you"
   There were no words
From an eight year old girl

CAROLINA HOLNESS
U.S. AIR FORCE, CONUS VETERAN

OMA DIED

1. Niels, Oma died...... Mom, I am getting deployed.

3. Please put your M-16 in the overhead compartment with the muzzle facing to the rear of the plane.

12. Release chaff... Fuck we haven't even arrived yet, and already we're getting shot at?

8. Wife? I don't know. Home? See previous question.

11. Alone. People say I'm not, but where are they then?

13a. Someone has been in my bedroom.

9. I can't believe you told everyone! What were you thinking? I was hurt... you don't understand.

4. 1st Casualty. Now it's on boys.
Fuck... it's been on since the first scud flew over.

5. At least I didn't really know him. There will be more.

7. Cross the border to Kuwait. Relief, breathe.
Two weeks later downtown Baghdad again; disillusioned.

2. We're taking the church bus to war.

13. No longer home, still alone.

6. GAS, GAS, GAS!!!!

15. I bought a shotgun, that wasn't smart.

16. I can't go back. I can't go back! PLEASE.

10. I wish I were dead.

18. I'm going to the morgue and overdose.

17. Going to drill exacerbates his symptoms.

20. Doig and Dorris and Wright are going back. Maybe I should?

14. I'm hurt. I'm weak.

19. Where have all my tears gone?

NIELS DAMMAN
U.S. ARMY, IRAQ VETERAN

GIRL

I cut my hair off the day before I left for basic training.
I hated it. I looked like a boy.
But all my friends said, "no you don't" or "it looks easy to take care of," but no one really said it looks good.

At MEPS, I walked by a group of guys (of course).
One of them yelled out, "Hey, what are you, a boy or a girl?"
I was mortified.

Basic was all girls and I figured out really quick, this hairdo was the best way to do it – so I actually got it cut shorter.

I was given a new identity. I'm not Mandy anymore, I'm Williams. There is no gender in a last name and there is no gender in the army. We are soldiers.

In AIT I started to let my hair grow out and then the senior drill instructor reminded me I'm not a soldier. I am a girl – in his own special way.

I was glad to get out of AIT and on with my military career.
But my first duty as a non-gendered soldier once I got to my permanent duty station was to get an abortion – December 27th, 1994. 18 ½ years old. 11 months away from home.

I don't know how to tell the story that continues. I feel like maybe you really don't want to know. Some of it sounds too outrageous. When do I tell too much? I wish I did not have this story. I wish I did not have these stories. I wish I did not have all of these fucking stories. But I do. So what do I do. If I am a soldier, then I become like the rest of them. Then maybe they see me as a solider and not as a girl.
How? Smoke, drink, cuss, tell dirty jokes, be the butt of the joke,

give them the same shit back. Be one of the guys. Push ups, sits ups, run, shoot good. Don't ask for help, don't whine, don't get sick, don't get the answer wrong. Be one of the guys.

I was pretty good at this. Maybe, maybe not. I guess at the end of the day, when I get in the shower, when I put on that bra, I am just a girl. Maybe I should learn to fight like one.

MANDY MARTIN
U.S. ARMY, IRAQ VETERAN

BEANS AND BULLETS

The briefing is over, maps and manifests in hand and mission understood: we must escort and protect another convoy of both military and civilian trucks to a remote base in need of "Beans and Bullets," at all costs.

Outside the wire, old Haj will be waiting with RPGs and IEDs in hand, waiting to burn those "beans" and explode those "bullets" which we had sworn to protect.

The word is given over the radio and the convoy rolls out; our gun trucks tactically spaced and weapons at ready. We roll along with eyes and gun-sights ever scanning and thoughts racing.

It is now 10:00 AM and 100 degrees as we approach a small town. It's always the same stench and sight; old broken vehicles and buildings, dust and garbage, and people milling about, either ignoring or gesturing at us. But today there are no people milling about, which means something is not right!!!!

Krack-Krack-Krack!!!! The sound and sensation of small arms fire rattling around us and then that oh-so-familiar sound and concussion of an IED going off alongside our convoy. Smoke and Flames rise and radios come alive.

The convoy stops and our gunners respond as crews dismount to provide security and assess the situation. Before me flames engulf what's left of the truck. Rounds and ammo inside the burning hulk cook-off adding another lethal aspect to this risky business of convoys.

Soon a medivac chopper arrives and carries off the casualties.

We then mount up our trucks and get ready to roll again. As I radio in with the other gun trucks, I notice the jubilant faces on emerging townspeople. Suddenly I grow cold and with weapon locked and loaded I start to raise my weapon, wanting to blast the smiles from the faces. But then I remember the "beans and bullets" that I swore to protect and the hungry "bellies and barrels" that would perish without them. I then give the order to move out.

And another convoy continues on......

JOSEPH HOLNESS
U.S. ARMY, IRAQ VETERAN

GOING IN COUNTRY

The training, the gear, the language you hear
Getting ready to go In Country

Enemy territory, planning, hating, convoys
Going In Country

Historical hate traveling from past to present calling enemy
territory Indian Country
In Country

Imbedded language so deep from the past that no one can hear
the hate anymore
On our way In Country

What side should I be on, I stare and wonder I look at them and
I see myself
In Country

Their brown skin matches mine – their drum, their smoke the
sage and the songs
Here I am In Country

This Indian is In Country—Indian Country
It feels familiar—does that make me then enemy?

Eli Painted Crow
U.S. Army, Iraq Veteran

THROUGH THE TURTLE'S EYES

The great river turtle stirs. What woke me up? A big boom. The ground is shaking. There's a terrible burning smell. I'm breathing smoke. The "uprights" are yelling.

"Lock and load! Dismount the trucks!"

Perhaps I'll just cruise down the stream to the river to see. Besides I can grab a tasty minnow or two while I'm at it—which will give me strength to master the river today.

The great turtle glides calmly towards the river. Hmmm... What is this movement and activity upon the land?

Diesel engines vibrating the ground as they idle in place. "We need a wrecker here! Get a wrecker here!"
Chains drag against metal.

Ahhh, yes. It's the uprights and the noisy land turtles fighting again. Here comes more uprights buzzing like angry bees.

"Halt! Stay back!"

What a terrible world for the uprights. Always fighting... always on the move... so much noise!

Why can't they be like us water turtles and enjoy the cool currents of the river or basking in the sun of the soft, sandy banks? I wonder if they ever gather like we do and just enjoy each others' company or dine peacefully on the river's delicacies.

How sad, well... I will leave them now to their bitter cycle of life. I must continue on with mine.

JOSEPH HOLNESS
U.S. ARMY, IRAQ VETERAN

IN A HOTEL ROOM IN TACOMA, WA

"Mandy, stop packing.
Stop.
Just stop.
Look at me.
Don't go. Let's just go home. I know you can leave this. I know
you don't have to go. It's me or the army. Marry me Mandy."

"I will not marry you under 'conditions.'
Sure I don't 'have' to go, but I have to go.
Being a soldier is the only thing I know how to be good at.
When you say 'I love you,' it means you love all of me—
not all of me except the soldier part.
That's like saying, 'I love all of you except for the artist part.'
So it sounds like to me you need to pack your shit cause I am not
leaving my soldiers for a man."

"I'm proud of you.

Let's do this—me and you.

Let me help you with that bag."

Mandy Martin
U.S. Army, Iraq Veteran

TRIGGERS - WAR UNWON

Futile occupation   Head full of lies
Hearts full of sorrow   Doesn't matter why
Mind full of memories   Living with danger
Bodies full of shrapnel   Fists full of anger
Got to blame someone for what's being done

Questions raised, as politicians scathe
Everyone is right while no one is wrong
Parents ask where their kids have gone
Peace lies in wait only at heavens gate
Lovers are torn and babies go unborn

Full of confusion   Environment unkind
Rules of engagement   Changing all the time
Abuse of detainees   Desecrated bodies
Do what you need to survive   No one cares for your life
Back home time to think   Guilt brings you to the brink
It's not easy, hero unsung
What's it worth when war in your head is unwon

ROBERT EATON
U.S. ARMY, VIETNAM VETERAN

OH PORTA SHITTER

Porta shitter, oh porta shitter
The other love of my life
My un-wielding companion,
You were always there for me
And there were many sides of my
Life that you served
You were an inviting toilet,
You were my secret lover
During lonely nights
Your body art was kind,
Your seductive stench sang out to me like a hot prom date
　　　God you were hot!
And your life was so simple, granted there was no plumbing yet
And I'm still sitting on my battle buddies shit.
I love not having to burn shit anymore, mixed with diesel, it's
filthy for sure.
The view was great once on the pot, but for all others
Involved, the view was not
　　　God, this thing is hot!!
I'm baking in my sweat and snot!
I hope these cramps will go away
So I don't have to sit here all damn day!

WE LOVE YOU KBR!!!!

Niels Damman & William Halfmoon
U.S. Army, Iraq Veterans

A SOLDIERS SON

Once upon a time in a land so far, far away there was a proud young soldier holding his newborn son. Witness to his first breath and flickering eyes opening to gaze upon his newborn father.

The father was a soldier and the son just a boy. The soldier father spoke of training, war and a duty to defend our country.

The boy was instructed along the way and encouraged to attend West Point upon reaching age; not to worry his appointment was secured.

So many years later in a land so far, far away a proud old soldier received a message.

The soldier had spent his life defending ideals, esprit de corps and an imagined way of life. The words of his life were simple: Duty, Honor, Country. Those three hallowed words reverently dictate what we can, will and must become. Always the soldier 1st, 2nd and last. The Core, The Core, The Core.

The message read: Your son joined the Army. He selected Infantry.

The old soldier's mind flashed to the charcoal bodies still steaming, to all those lifeless bodies he stepped over throughout the years. The ghostly memories of those who gave all to follow the soldier's path. Their smiles, the spark in their eyes, their hopes and dreams and sons so far away.

For the soldier knew he killed his son. Not by enemy fire, but ideals and dreams of the soldier father. For the son had placed his tiny feet into his father's heavily worn boots, not because he wanted to become a soldier. Far deeper it was, for the son only wanted to feel his father's love. He innocently tried to follow in his soldier father's impossible path. Out of Duty, Honor and Obligation.

The Soldier replied: Do not come, this path you cannot follow. But the reply came to late. The son was already training, a Ranger accepted to Special Forces, a soldiers soldier was he to be.

The soldier received a message in a land so far away.
The message read: Sir your son is gone. BREAK.
The soldier replied: Last message over. Clarify, where is my son? BREAK.
Sir, we do not know, we think he is AWOL, they say he refuses to return to unit. Silence---Not possible---DESERTER! UNTHINKABLE!! Betrayal of ideals... sorrow.

The old soldier's battle scars began to hurt, his armor fell crashing at his feet. Stabbed from within. Where so many enemy failed, the son prevailed, piercing the soldier's Achilles. Shattered ideals, a young lamb raised as sacrifice for the dreams of the soldier father.

In a land so far, far away a final digital message read as follows: Dad, your path I will not follow. Love... your son.
The old soldier replied: I deserted my son... OUT.

KEN KRAFT
U.S. ARMY, IRAQ VETERAN

COMING BACK ON ME

Verse 1
They're coming home feelin' all alone,
Thousand yard stare no one there.
They want to tell about it and no one cares.
Happened once before in a far off land was a nightmare called Vietnam
Now I see it all happening again—got my mind in a spin.

Verse 2
Going are the soldiers of the great war,
Korea and Nam we stand at the door.
And everyday I see the young faces of the Gulf wars.
Claiming their places in a long line,
memories of war are so unkind.
Powers that be, why can't you see
you just can't win a war with no end.

Chorus
I watch it all from afar, the time is different but not the war.
Thought I had it all behind me, but watching this war,
it's coming back on me.
Coming back on me, like wind on the desert and waves on the sea.
Just can't stop those old war memories from coming back on me.

Verse 3
We gave with all our might, never ran from battle,
we never lost a fight.
Now here they are proud as can be,
looking for help from you and me,
lost in this world feeling alone,
dreams about a war trying to find their way home.
And when these Gulf Vets I see, I look in they're eyes and I see me

Verse 4

How many faces must I see suffer the pain of war with me?
Gone is our childhood, gone for good.
And when I think of how I was treated and now it's being repeated
All I can do is cry all alone and pray the troops will all safely
come home.

Chorus

I watch it all from afar, the time is different but not the war.
Thought I had it all behind me, but watching this war,
it's coming back on me.
Coming back on me when will it end the guilt and the shame it's
back again
Coming back on me won't you let me be that old war it still
haunts me.

ROBERT EATON
U.S. ARMY, VIETNAM VETERAN

PRESCHOOL

FOB ... RPG ... IED ... TBI ...

PTSD ... ICU ...   MEB ...   PEB ...

GWB ...   U ... SOB ...

NEXT TIME DON'T

F – U – C – K ...   USA!

RORY DUNN
U.S. ARMY, IRAQ VETERAN
AND
CYNTHIA LEFEVER
MOTHER OF RORY DUNN

PROCEDURE

In 1969 I was an eighteen year old medic and found myself detached to the 67th Evac Hospital in Vietnam. I'm going to describe step by step a common procedure I carried out while working on the I.C.U.

1) Remove all tubes from the body
2) Pack gauze into the holes to prevent leakage of body fluids on their way home
3) Tie the penis off and pack the anus with gauze
4) Tie the right hand over the left and place on the stomach
5) Tie the jaws shut
6) Pack gauze into the nostrils and ears
7) Tie the right foot over the left and tie the body tag on the right big toe
8) Finally with reverence and somebody helping – place the body in the body bag

At first I body-bagged the Vietnamese with the same reverence, but only several weeks, after body-bagging so many G.I.s, I could grab a gook by the shirt, hair—whatever and throw them into their bags. As a side note: when I got sober I did the 4th of the 12 steps of Alcoholics Anonymous, made a fearless moral inventory of myself, and it was the last time I called a Vietnamese a gook. I used it only for emphasis.

I didn't work in graves registration where they bagged people they didn't know. The boys I put in those bags I had also taken care of as patients on the ward. I got to know these kids: while bathing, shaving, changing dressings, and feeding etc…

We would talk about their families, where they lived, about their fears.

Well, I have no idea how many young men, brave soldiers, I put into those bags. At the end of six months I refused to do any more.

Now I do it in my sleep.

MIKE SCHENK
U.S. ARMY, VIETNAM VETERAN

THE HALLS OF KNOWING

Walk the halls
Walk the halls with your eyes open
And you will begin
To know the truth of it

Look at each of them
Don't be afraid
They are still the same

Look into their eyes
If they are still there
Look into their hearts
If they aren't

Look at their missing limbs
They already know
You can't avoid it
They already know

Look at their burns, their scars
They already know
You can't avoid it
They already know

Changed forever
But still the same

Husband
Wife
Father
Son
Mother
Daughter
Brother
Sister
They are changed forever
But still the same...

STAN LEFEVER
STEP-FATHER OF RORY DUNN

LIMA CHARLIE

Dear god in heaven, or wherever,
Perhaps because my humvee rolls through the valleys of the
shadow of death --
>Tagab,
>Jalalabad,
>Kabul,
Or perhaps because this land looks so much like the picture bible
of my childhood,
I look for you in its swirling sands.
Any of these mounts, it seems, could hold a Jesus
Preaching blessings on all that I am not --
>the meek,
>the peacemaker.

I went to three chaplains with my cloven soul.
The first one gave me medals of your saints,
>Michael with his sword,
>(they're fond of that one.)
The second anointed my head with oil,
But couldn't tell me why my cup runneth over
When all around me your children die for want of drink,
Their thirsty bodies too weak to scream,
Whispering your name.
The third offered holy water to douse me with,
While just outside two babies were sprinkled
with shrapnel.

From minarets they call out your greatness,
But the explosions drown their prayers, seeming greater still.
Mortars steal children.
Rockets crumble men.
"If any should die before they wake..."
(Well, you know the rest, I'm sure.)

The bombs rain down. Fire from above.
The mines, like geysers. Fire from below.
And in the streets the fires are burning.

We speak of fighting fire with fire,

Of firefights, firepower,
Enemy fire and friendly.

I plead with you for cleansing fire.
The candles burning on a million altars,
Smoldering incense, sage, or sweetgrass
Exhaling over the world.

Couldn't a monk set himself ablaze or something?
(It seems fitting now.)

Or the one I was taught to call Prince of Peace
Could send his spirit down in tongues of flame.
(A dove would work as well, I suppose, the symbolism lost on
no one.)

The Cherokee and Navajo burn sacred tobacco to find you.
I, for my part, flick my seventeenth cigarette against a bush,
Hoping it may ignite and you might speak.

The brush catches for a moment, crackles, then dissolves into
silence.
Like static on a radio:

Agnus Dei, qui tolis pecata mundi,
Miserere nobis. How copy, over?

Agnus Dei, qui tolis pecata mundi,
Miserere nobis. How copy, over?

Agnus Dei, qui tolis pecata mundi,
Dona nobis pacem.

The silence on your end thunders in my skull,
So deafeningly
            loud
               and clear.

Laura Carpenter
U.S. Army, Afghanistan Veteran

PURPLE HEART

My brother has one
In a box in a drawer
In a bottle, at the pawn shop

Dan Shea
USMC Vietnam Veteran

Michael was on an operation in which he was one of some 17 men in our platoon that survived and Mike was sent home in a straightjacket. We are both haunted by our experiences he more so than me and it is killing him.

NOT ANOTHER LINE

Please don't ask me
to write another poem—not another line
about Viet Nam
not about war
or how I feel
about Iraq and Afghanistan.

It sucks man
It fuckin' sucks.

If you want to
know how I feel
go put your fuckin' shit
on the line
and you won't have to ask!

Dan Shea
USMC, Vietnam Veteran

AGENT ORANGE

Agent Orange
Agent Blue
Agent Fuckin' Pink
Colors on barrels
With skull & cross bones
Children...
Bodies twisted and maimed
Vietnamese & mine
Now we have something in common

DAN SHEA
USMC, VIETNAM VETERAN

Dan Shea had a child born with multiple birth defects, congenital heart disease, cleft palate, prune belly... Casey was born 12/16/77 and died post heart surgery after 7 weeks in a coma on 2/25/81

MAGGOTS AND GOLD

Create a village as strong as a war
To pick the maggots off my skin
And burnish the gold that lies within
This will renew the strength of my sacred core.
Can we create a village as strong as a war?

JACK MCLEAN
USMC, VIETNAM VETERAN

ON THE DEATH OF A YOUNG SUICIDE BOMBER

He tried to kill my best friend.
He was enemy.
He was dead.

I know how I was supposed to feel,
But still I cannot muster any wry laughter for this man
Whose corpse and car bomb are now cool, silent, still.

The nightmares lie to me.
If Freud was right, and our dreams reveal our wishes,
Then I must wish his body were merely dismantled,
Strewn about in wayward bits someone might come along to
Frankenstein together.

I see it all when I sleep:
Limbs torn from torso cleanly, like puzzle pieces,
Entrails tumbling out the belly uncoiled, but intact,
Still-moist viscera glistening in the Afghan sun.

It isn't true.
Nothing was left whole.

His clothing, white cotton streaked with blood and shit,
Clung to the mangled steel in strips,
Like bandages dressing a giant metal wound.
Sand-colored dogs, marred with gore, tore flesh from carcass.

And all around, the pulp of him.

Like kitchen waste left out too long,
Stinking in the street.

I know they promised him glory.
We are all promised glory.
They must have told him he was off to save the world from evil,
Kindled some righteous fire inside the membranes that split that
day

To release, all around, the pulp of him.

The sticky softness,
The juice.

I think of my own body,
Which seemed so solid a moment before,
A frame for armor, ammo, rifle,
A vessel filled with strength.

But I saw, all around, the pulp of him.

Human batter,
Baking in the heat.

And I think of the body of my own son,
As he grows in the shadow of Ft. Bragg, Pope Air Force Base,
Camp LeJeune.
Soon there will be G.I. Joes and little green Army men, I know.
And an Xbox to spray pixillated carnage in his face,
And movies to teach him which people are "good guys" and
which are killable.
The recruiters will come.
They'll promise glory once again.
There will be no human batter in the ads.
No sticky softness.
No kitchen waste.

I think of him asleep in peace,
For he has no nightmares of war to interfere.
I want to still the gunfire, the bombs, the soldiers' chants,
That goddamned soul-stripping wry laughter,
And the naked malice they told me I should feel.

I want to still them all and say:
        Hush now, world,
        A child is sleeping,
        A sweet soufflé still rising,
        So desperately fragile.

        And if you must use words
                like martyr and infidel
                or hero and enemy,
        Then whisper them.
        It is all too easy to destroy.

A clotted mess of protein in the bottom of the pan.
A brown-red stain soaking into dust.

LAURA CARPENTER
U.S. ARMY, AFGHANISTAN VETERAN

SUCK IT UP

Necrotic tissue   job almost done
Not much left
Mostly just a hole now

SUCK IT UP!!

PAIN SORROW DIVORCE SUICIDE ANGER AND
RAGE LOSS GRIEF DEATH DISABILITY

SUCK IT UP!!!!

I can't hear or listen anymore
The ears and eyes are working but I can not hear and there is no
place to go
Capacity is gone and I must move on

SUCK IT UP!!!!!!!

Come on maggots, do your FUCKING JOB!
Let's get to the gold
Cause you know
It is heal or die

SUCK IT UP

Michael J. Maxwell, MS
Combat Veteran Counselor

II

The Heart Is A Bridge

SOUND BYTES...

Hello . . .

Yes . . .

Mother . . .

Captain . . .

Roadside . . .

Cannot say . . .

Sustained . . .

Don't know . . .

Fallujah – Baghdad – Landstuhl
Critical – Open – Head – Trauma

Our boy . . .

Aisle or window seat?

CYNTHIA LEFEVER
MOTHER OF RORY DUNN

CCAT

How to you transport a body that has been broken
Almost beyond repair
How do you keep them alive when you can't bring a hospital along

It seems so crude
A stretcher?
Wood and canvas
Not even a gurney?

Don't drop him!

Machines suspended over the legs
Monitor – what do all the lines mean?
Alarms often sounding
Ventilator – its slow, sickening click - hisssssss
Click - hisssss
IV bags hanging over
Strange inflated bags too
What do they do?

A team of people make the move
Nurse
Anesthesiologist
I hope there is a doctor

Bags and bags of gear
For whatever may happen
With no hospital around

Unhook him
Rehook him
Quick!
Now on the move
A bus

An airplane
Nightingale

No seats
Stretchers suspended from straps from ceiling to floor
Stacked 4 high
Swinging haphazardly
This is how our wounded heroes come home

Web seats for those who can use them
Wounded warriors everywhere
Returning home

The CCAT patients load last
No stacking them
In a sleep so deep
They need constant care
Small dignity for these naked, broken warriors
A priest among them

5 CCATs today
5 bodies who cannot even breath for themselves

They say 2 flights a week
10 brave men and women like this every week?

How do they do it
The CCAT teams
Back and forth across the pond
Ferrying the almost dead home
And never knowing who lives and who dies...

STAN LEFEVER
STEP-FATHER OF RORY DUNN

ROAD MARCH

Don't get me wrong – I know it was a dream
DO NOT get me wrong – I know it was a dream
        NOT!
My dream went like this:
In the middle of the night, I sat up in the dark
And opened my eyes to see what was there
Don't get me wrong – this was an ordinary,
middle-of-the-night dream
DO NOT get me wrong – this was an ordinary,
middle-of-the-night dream
        NOT!
This what I saw:
A soldier in camo on a dirt road
Without moving his feet, he marched to the foot of my bed
I saw he was young and strong and so very handsome
I saw his camo was clean with the collar starched
I looked down and saw his desert boots were new without a
single stain
I looked up again and now saw only half of a face and one empty
eye socket

Without speaking any words, I asked him what he wanted
Without moving his lips, he telegraphed back:
        Be MY Mom
Without moving his arms, he showed me his clean hands with
no blood or dirt under his nails
Without moving his arms, he reached for me as he telegraphed
another plea:
Bring ME Home

I closed my eyes or maybe I just blinked
When a twin appeared by his side

Young and strong and handsome
Clean and starched with an identical half face and empty eye
socket
Together without moving, with no signs of blood or gore, with
no tears
The twins reached for me as they telegraphed:
        Be OUR Mom, Bring US Home

I blinked again and then there were four marching in a row
I blinked again and then there were eight marching with four in
a row
Then 16 with 4 to a row, Then 32 with 4 to a row
The road filled with half faces and empty eye sockets

Silently and respectfully, without moving, they marched on that
dirt road at the foot of my bed
Until I heard their souls and their Purple Hearts start to roar
They telegraphed in unison:

        Be OUR Mom
        FOR GOD'S SAKE, BRING US HOME!

CYNTHIA LEFEVER
MOTHER OF RORY DUNN

WHO, WHAT, WHERE, WHEN, WHY

Who: Mike Hastie (That's me)

What: War

Where: Vietnam (U.S. Army Medic)

When: September 1970 to September 1971

Why: Sorry, that's political, and we don't want to talk about that. Whenever the truth threatens one's belief system, there is a strong tendency to deny its reality.
The Vietnam Veterans Memorial in Washington, D.C. is 150 yards long.
58,000 American soldiers were killed in Vietnam. Their average age was 19-- from the senior prom to Vietnam. The vast majority were from working class, and poor families.

Why: How many times have I heard, " That's the way it has always been."
Politicians who start wars, never go, nor do they ever send their own children.
But, that's politics, and that is called a free pass, as in freedom. Before I forget, let me get back to the Vietnam Veterans Memorial in Washington, D.C. If the same kind of wall were built for the Vietnamese, who were killed in Their country, with the same density of names, that wall would be nine miles long.

Nine years after I got back from Vietnam, I found myself in a padded cell of a psychiatric hospital, because I was so filled with rage and depression. The betrayal of the Vietnam War almost destroyed me. Betrayal is like a bounty hunter, it can scare you to death. I felt tossed away like a paper cup after a movie. When you follow the money trail, you always find out the truth.

Lying Is The Most Powerful Weapon In War.

I came back from Vietnam in 1971. Fast-forward to 2008, and the lies of the Vietnam War, started the Iraq War. It is all a dog and pony show. War profiteering in Iraq, is beyond the human imagination. When you see an American soldier take his or her last breath, and you find no justification for it, your belief system is changed forever.

On day while I was in a bunker in Vietnam, a sniper round went over my head. The person who fired that weapon was not a terrorist, a rebel, an extremist, or a so-called insurgent. The Vietnamese individual who tried to kill me was a citizen of Vietnam, who did not want me in His country.
This truth escapes millions.

MIKE HASTIE
U.S. ARMY MEDIC, VIETNAM VETERAN

I AM

I am not pro-war, anti-war, pro-Bush, anti-Bush. I AM a soldier, I AM a warrior.

I AM a deployable instrument used to project force, power and freedom, bound by oath to protect, defend our constitution and way of life.

My responsibility is great, my sorrows even greater. I have walked through the Valley of Death and camped within its borders. Others passed my camp on their final journey. Some were comrades and parts of me traveled with them.

All alive pass through the Valley, past my camp. Some will stroll by happily, while others travel with great sorrow and pain. I volunteered and asked to enter. I am trapped between. I exited the Valley but was sent back to tend the camp a while longer, exiled of my own accord.

Forgiveness, acceptance are all things to consider before your journey. Redemption is not found within the Valley walls.

I have the coffee brewing, stop by if you are lost. I'll show you the path. But the direction you follow is up to you.

KEN KRAFT
U.S. ARMY, IRAQ VETERAN

BALANCING THE BOOKS

A Soldier Boy
    A new husband
A Soldier Boy
    A new dad
My Soldier Boy
    A new recruit
My Soldier Boy
    21 with zero dependents
My Soldier Boy
    A Volunteer: "I'll go on ahead first to meet"

The Daisy-Chained, Roadside, Improvised Explosive Device . . .

My Soldier Boy
    Medivaced
My Soldier Boy
    On life support
My Soldier Boy
    Cannot return to duty

Fucking Army Surgeon General
    "Get him off the books"

Your Soldier Boy?
    A new recruit?

                                    CYNTHIA LEFEVER
                                    MOTHER OF RORY DUNN

BEING LOST

Being lost is no fun
No exaggeration for some
But since the Nam
It's been the norm.

No longer do I have a country I can trust.
They lied and said we were there
to stop the communist thrust.
The war became survival
Not for God or country did we kill.

Being lost is no fun.
Can God forgive me?
The Book says yes… but for me?
Every day I think about Vietnam
Whether from helicopter, smell, or a song.

Being lost is no fun.

MIKE SCHENK
U.S. ARMY, VIETNAM VETERAN

THE BETRAYAL

Shattered lives, crying mothers, sisters and wives for all the lost lives

Broken hearts, lost body parts, don't know where to start

Hollow eyes, quiet sighs, knowing we live a lie

You thank me for my service and it really makes me nervous

Because I don't feel proud and I can't stand the sound of "thank you"

I speak this truth to Power and I take a stand in stride

Because you can run but you cannot hide and I will speak about your genocide

We the soldiers are not to blame

For all the lost lives in your war game

We were born of lives for many tribes died for this nation to rise

Now we all know betrayal

ELI PAINTED CROW
U.S. ARMY, IRAQ VETERAN

LITTLE BROTHER

He knew how
To push my buttons
And followed me
Into the Marines
And to Vietnam

He took my place
And probably saved my life
Alive among the dead
They sent him home in a strait jacket

We share the pain
We share a history of family
His wounds are deeper than mine
I just want him to know
How much I love him
But god dammit, wish you
Had just left me alone

Dead among the living

      Love
       Bro

DAN SHEA
USMC, VIETNAM VETERAN

My brother Michael joined at the same time, we were in boot-camp together, Mike signed a waiver and somehow was stationed in the same company as me in Vietnam. I was sent out of country and about four months later Michael was on an operation in which he was one of some 17 men in our platoon that survived and was sent home in a straightjacket. We are both haunted by our experiences he more so than me and it is killing him.

UNTITLED

This Wednesday while seeing my therapist.
I heard him say he thought I was in shock.
I'd never thought about it before.

I heard a man in this room talk about his abusive
father and how he had to always be aware of what his
father was doing because he didn't know if/when he would snap.
This same man spoke of betrayal.

As I sat in the back of the room
my healing tears started to roll down my cheeks –

I realized my life was more similar than different.
I knew I was meant to be here at this time.

As I hear the voices in this room I feel
I'm not alone in my war.

DEBORAH GUERRERO
FRIEND OF ELI PAINTED CROW

SWEET DREAMS

I am exhausted,
maybe the beer will kick in when I lay my head down on
the pillow.
The TV keeps saying the same shit about nothing and I'm out of
beer anyway.
Clock says 12:30. Gotta work tomorrow.

Mandy.
You gotta get up off the couch. It's only sleep.
They are only dreams. Stop being a chicken shit and get up.
Be quiet, don't wake anyone. Crawl into bed or pick up some
Tim O'Brien.
Maybe reading of the things they carried will help me with the
things I carry.
I can't read it. I keep reading the same sentence over and over.
I don't know what it says.

Fuck it, just try.

But what if I have another one.
If I stop thinking about it maybe I can fall asleep.
I forgot to check on Katrina.
She's ok. She's ok. She's ok.
What's the noise? If my brain would shut the fuck up maybe I
could hear it.
What is it? My heart is beating to loud Still can't hear it.
I gotta look. Don't wake anyone up.
It's close, it's in the house? It's outside?
It's close. Right across the hall?
Shhh. Open the door slowly. Don't wake her.
She can't hear it but it's right outside her window.
That damn rose bush rubbing against the window—right?

Just peek. You have to check, it's the only way to sleep—
just check.
Pull the curtains just a crack. It's dark. It's moving.
It's closer, he's wearing white, like a dress.
He's dark, he's Hajji.
Don't let him see me. Save her. Turn around.
Go back to the bedroom. Get the shotgun.
Go. Go. Go. Go.
Unlock the fucking thing.
Go. Go. Go. Go.
Get to the room.
Oh fuck there he.
Find some beer and try again?

MANDY MARTIN
U.S. ARMY, IRAQ VETERAN

TO BE ACCEPTED FOR THE JOB I DID IN IRAQ

The trip started in January 2004. I know this because that is my birthday and I was 49. I was told I was going to work for the Army. I am in the Air Force Reserve.

When I got to Iraq I worked nights at ADAC off-loading cargo from the C5's and C17's. I worked the night shift and lived in a tent with other airmen working the day shift. When they weren't out on convoys, they were in the tent making noise all day long. That sucked because I didn't get any sleep.

The rest of the company thought that I did not have a real job because I did not leave the base and was not shot at or hit with RPG's, or mortars, or rockets working on the flight line.

The base is nicknamed "mortar capital of Iraq." The main target was the planes on the flight line. My main job was to live through the attacks on the flight line. The other job was to deliver cargo to eight distribution stops on the base without getting shot at or hit by an RPG.

When I was getting "short" one of the friends I made in Iraq got home and shot himself with his own M-16.

When I got home I expected to see someone from my base at the airport. No one came. I felt abandoned by the US Airforce.

I was ignored by most everybody on the base. I felt that I was being treated as if I had the plague.

Being accepted for the job I did in Iraq.

DANIEL NIELSEN
U.S. AIR FORCE, IRAQ VETERAN

IT'S OUR TIME DOWN HERE

2000 puzzle pieces tossed in the air.
How do you catch them all?
You grab some,
Sometimes you're on your game and you grab a whole handful.
Then the next time THAT hand reaches for just one piece, it drops all the rest,
Drops the rest and doesn't get the one.

IT'S JUST A PUZZLE! Why is it so hard?
I did puzzles as a child and NOW I can't?!

Puzzles aren't done in the sky….in mid air.
They are done on stable flat ground.
The only way to collect all the pieces is to let them all fall.
Collect on the ground.
There they are, down there.
The only way to pick them up is to get on my knees, LIKE A BITCH.
I have to cower on my knees in order to pick up the pieces.
I can't do that.
I wont submit.
So I'll squat down and do the puzzle on m lap.
But that doesn't work.
The pieces are all here, but now they wont stay together.
The support under them is too soft.
I have them all here.
I can see them.
I have control of them now, but they wont what I want, or stay where I put them.
So they fall back to the floor and I have lost them again.
What if I am tired and need to rest?
I will just sit down for a while?

The perspective is different down here.
My eyes adjust and it's not so bad.
But I wont get on my knees is submission.

From here I am closer to the floor.
I see the pieces of the unknown picture scattered around me.

If I lean down I can pick a few up, but not all of them.
I want to see the picture so badly.
I think it will show me the key to my life … my direction.

I can't take it any more!
I have to see what it is.

So I surrender.
So lost, my spirit is broken and I get on my knees,
And START, begrudgingly, to put the pieces together.

One corner is done and I think I can predict the rest of the
picture.
I am so excited and I jump up to start THAT life,
The life I see in the corner that I have put together.

But I am too tired.
I can't even sit.
I have to lay down.
I just want to close my eyes for a minute.

I am back on my knees…but only in transition to laying down.
"You are weak for laying down….for resting."
"What do you do?" People ask,
"Anything I want." I tell them
It sounds better than "I'm unemployed and can't hold a job!"

I take a breath while I lay.
There are my puzzle pieces.
I roll over and from my resting place,
I can begin to put my pieces together.

Now I have the border done, and that one corner from before.
I am excited about the rest of the picture,
I can't wait to see it.
So I stay laying down.
Up on my elbows, feet waving back and forth, ankles crossing in mid-air.
This is how we used to do puzzles as kids.
On the floor, feet waving in the air,
Saturday and Sunday....all day, sometimes all summer long,
Maintained by the joy of seeing the picture
And the accomplishment of finding the pieces...
One at a time.

MELISSA STEINMAN
U.S. COAST GUARD, KUWAIT VETERAN

WARRIOR

How do you live in a land where those who rule ask so
much from you and expect it in an honorable and trustworthy
manner; yet "they" who make such demands have forgotten
what honor and trust really are.

It's frustrating and many times enraging;
but the ones from whom so much is asked
should always remember that when called upon
to give it their all or ultimate sacrifice,
that it is carried out by those who really are the honorable
and trustworthy of the land.

JOSEPH HOLNESS
U.S. ARMY, IRAQ VETERAN

ODE TO RORY

Rory Dunn was blown up by a roadside bomb on his 22nd birthday, 5-26-2004, and suffered traumatic brain injury, the loss of his right eye, and blinded in his left eye.

He lost his hearing and part of his skull and still carries shrapnel in his head and suffers from PTSD. Two of his best friends were killed along side of him. His struggle to survive was further complicated by the military machine upon his return to Walter Reed. The military's priority was to be rid of this wounded hero. Rory and his mom and dad advocate for the wounded warriors to be treated with respect and dignity until they have recovered enough to return to society.

I had the opportunity to meet this young man at our retreat to welcome home veterans of wars and was profoundly effected by him and his family's courage. This song is for you Rory.

chorus
The Generals come in says we'll shed a tear
Just as soon as you sign this paper right here
They'll be tears of joy that we don't have to share
The cost of the pain you will forever bear

verse
Fallujah, Iraq and another sunny day
Time to go out for the grim game we play
We're loaded for bear and ready to kill
But today the killing will be on our bill
Flash of fire and the last sound I hear
Are the sounds of my friends as they leave this earth
And so I die but before I awake again
The smell of death is burned into my brain
Silent sounds from those who provide care
And though I can't hear the screaming is still there

chorus
Then the Generals come in says we'll shed a tear
Just as soon as you sign this paper right here
They'll be tears of joy that we don't have to share
The cost of the pain you will forever bear

verse

Best friends blown apart in Fallujah, Iraq
Why am I the only one to come back
Wives left alone with a folded flag
A child with a medal and no memory of dad
They're spirit lives on within me
Forever grateful I will always be
I joke and I laugh to numb the pain
Gets me through the day as it happens over and over again
My body is mangled and full of the war
Sometimes I feel I can't give anymore, then the

chorus

Generals come in says we'll shed a tear
Just as soon as you sign this paper right here
They'll be tears of joy that we don't have to share
The cost of the pain you will forever bear

verse

Makes more courageous to stand up and fight
For the wounded warriors hell and their plight
Left to waste away in a hospital bed
Promises of glory the generals said
As the generals take advantage of our war inside
And offer us promises and belittle our pride
Pinning on medals with much fanfare
While secretly planning how to get us out of there
I will fight for my country on my own shores
until our young soldiers have to fight no more

chorus

And when Generals come in saying we'll shed a tear
Just as soon as you sign this paper right here
I'll be shedding tears of joy that the soldiers won't fear
Saying no to the Generals standing there.

ROBERT EATON
U.S. ARMY, VIETNAM VETERAN

POEM

There is a poem
I started to write
A long, long time ago

I just couldn't get it right,
because I wanted to say,
I wanted to tell
I wanted to witness
—see I just can't get it right.

It's an old poem
the words are in
an ancient language
you don't need
an interpreter
everyone understand

It's a new poem
It will change your life
It fuckin' changed me
And I haven't even written it yet.

It's not about Vietnam
but it is
It's not about Iraq
but it is

How can I tell you about the pain,
the scars of war?
How can I fucking get you to hear what I'm writing?
Will you feel my pain?
Will you hear the screams I hear in the night?
Will you wake-up in the middle of the night?
Will you see the faces of the children I have seen?

It's an old poem
It's a new poem
It should be the last poem!

DAN SHEA
USMC, VIETNAM VETERAN

III

Home and the After-math

DREAD IT

First, I am an engineer, and generally engineers don't make good poets…

Second, I am a civilian and not a veteran. I am here with my wife Cynthia and with our son Rory who was critically injured in Iraq 4 years ago today. Since that time, my family and I have been for a time immersed in the military medical system, and more recently working extensively with injured veterans and their families…

Over the four years since our son was injured I have spent a great deal of time around military personnel. Officers, enlisted, male, female, young, old, many different races. Some physically wounded, emotionally wounded, spiritually wounded, or not wounded (at least to their conscious awareness). In this time the respect that I have always held for those who have served our country has grown into a reverence. As a group these individuals have no parallel. They are dedicated, skilled, loyal, proud, and so many more adjectives than I have at my disposal. They have all served their country, and I have come to fiercely believe that each civilian in this country owes them, and every service member who has gone before them, a debt of gratitude for our very way of life.

Also in this time I have witnessed some of the best and greatest the human spirit has to offer (as well as some of the worst). People have come out of nowhere to offer and provide support to those at greatest need. Whether volunteer, medical professional, friend, neighbor, or complete stranger, you just never know. For me, most of all, I have seen the strength of the human spirit in the will to survive demonstrated by my son, who found joy and laughter in his heart even during his darkest hours, and in my wife, who would and will stop at nothing to assist her son and now so many others at finding and getting what they need to continue on their journey to recovery…

I am somewhat saddened at the fact that I used to watch war movies, and enjoy them. Don't get me wrong, I was able to comprehend in my head what war was about. I was fully aware that war is not all about valor, glory, and victory. I knew in my head that it was about pain, and suffering, and death. The engineer in me could even calculate the terrible forces and energies involved, and what it might do to a human body, but that is all physical. What I could not comprehend in this head of mine is the emotional and spiritual trauma of war, because that, in my view, cannot be calculated or comprehended… it can only be felt. And that is what has happened to me. Over the past four years in this world I never knew before, having heard so much about what war really is, first hand, from those who have been there, my mental comprehension of what war must be like has grown into a very tangible feeling in my heart. And that feeling in my heart fills me with dread. Dread for what so many have experienced, what so many are experiencing right now, today. And dread for what so many will experience tomorrow, next month, and the month after that if we do not change course. We should not go about their daily lives without understanding that there is a war going on each and every day, and the unimaginable sacrifices that are being made for each of us each and every day. You will hear of some of these sacrifices tonight, from those who have made them…

Very little of this attracts the attention of the national media. Wonder that? It isn't pretty. Much of it is ugly. But we need to hear it. We need to feel it. It is but a small piece of the reality of war.

One thing I want to make absolutely clear. Although I now believe I have some ability to truly feel in my heart what war must do to those who are in it, I absolutely know that I DO NOT UNDERSTAND war. I do not understand war in my gut. That is reserved only for those individuals, heads, hearts, and souls, who have put their lives on the line in combat.

My thanks to you all wherever you are.

STAN LEFEVER
STEP-FATHER OF RORY DUNN

XO, OPERATIONS, FORCE PROTECTION

2200 Soldiers, civilians—men, women, husbands, wives, sons, daughters, brothers, sisters, moms, dads...

All those dreams, hopes, uncertain futures, thrown together in an unfamiliar land with cultures as old as time recorded. My role was that of leader, follower and servant to those under my leadership.

We had a large farewell celebration and talked of times past and a future homecoming. The conversations fading in and out like static on the radio. I swelled with pride with the thought of serving my country and serving with so many brave young men and women.

Then everyone left, except my wife and I. We began saying our goodbyes, stalling, trying to find words. Each time she left the room I cried, only to quickly wipe the tears away. Then the time came to say goodbye. We hugged and embraced with tears. We watched each other part, one walking down the ramp to the plane, the other standing alone.

My new role was to care for all those young men and women.

Each morning I would look into their eyes, ask how they were doing, ask about home, equipment, and how their NCO's were treating them. Each one in my mind throughout the day; at sunset upon return, I again repeated the process. My days were 18 hours 7 days a week.

I could not eat or sleep and still have trouble throughout the night.

I kept their pictures on the wall to remind me of each loss and cling to our conversations and pray that I did all I could. I thought of all those they left standing alone watching them make that walk down the ramp.

I naively promised to grieving family members that I would bring their wife and husband home.

Right. That's a promise only GOD could make, but it seemed to be the right thing to comfort them.

When returning home with them alive I felt as if I carried unbelievable weight. They thanked me, I cried.

I walked up my ramp alone—to a reception of none. There was no welcome home party, because like so many others I'm not home.

KEN KRAFT
U.S. ARMY, IRAQ VETERAN

I WEAR A BUTTON

I wear a button
Veterans for Peace
Somebody asks
What war were you in?

Vietnam
So was my brother, my mother,
My sister, my husband,
My son, my wife, my dad.

I'll ask how is
he or she doing.
He died in country,
She died of breast cancer
just last year.
He's homeless, drunk or in jail.
She works at the VA.
He teaches, she sings

It's a mix of questions
And responses but maybe
My button should say there is
"No Peace for Veterans".

DAN SHEA
USMC, VIETNAM VETERAN

BAGHDAD SANDS

Baghdad sands like the sands of time
Forever sifting through my mind
Don't want to go back but
Baghdad sands won't let go

When I'm walking through the crowds
My mind going wild
Don't be afraid it's alright
Baghdad sands storming through my mind

Oh, they all say I must make my way
You fought for the land and the country owes you man
But I've lost my youth so what's the use
Baghdad sand blowing through my mind

So I sit and wonder why
Tears won't come, don't even try
Just passing time, time is mine
Baghdad sands flowing through my mind

Well, Baghdad sands like the sands of time
Forever sifting across my mind
Don't want to go back but
Baghdad sands won't let go

Robert Eaton
U.S. Army, Vietnam Veteran

DID I MENTION THE WAR GAVE ME PTSD?

The sky is blue

I am blue

God I hope you aren't to.

Did I mention the war gave me PTSD?

But that's enough about me.

The grass is green

Many days I don't want to be seen.

The water is cold

I am cold.

The night is black

Did I mention I fought in Iraq?

They brought my broken body back

But left my Mind's Eye in Iraq.

Did I mention the war gave me PTSD?

The moon is bright

I don't sleep at night.

Man that girl in the 2nd rows ass is tight.

Did I mention the war gave me PTSD?

KEN KRAFT
U.S. ARMY, IRAQ VETERAN

FUCK

I'm just getting teared up.
Since my flashback my world has been numb.
Turned upside down.
I had to put my doggy down who has been by my side
for 13 years.
I haven't been able to cry.
It just won't come.

We heard a story that mentioned
maggots being cleaned off the noble man.
The whole village came to help that noble man.
The maggots cleaning the dead tissue leaving way
for growth of new flesh and
the gold to take hold and spreading the healing process.
Always remember,
PTSD will always be there
but we can learn to understand it and therefore live with it.

MIKE SCHENK
U.S. ARMY, VIETNAM VETERAN

SECOND/HAND PTSD
BY THE WIFE OF A DISABLED VIETNAM VET

You all have heard about the dangers of 2nd hand smoke. Well, my story's about 2nd hand PTSD. My husband has suffered from PTSD since he was 19 years old and after fighting two tours in an ugly war called Vietnam. Of course, he didn't know he had it—and neither did I.

When I first met him, it was love at first sight --for both of us. He moved in with me right away. Ten months later came our baby boy. Then we got married. I found out that's the way they do it in California—first honeymoon, then baby, then marriage. The first year together was lovey-dovey, lovey-dovey all the time. But as the years passed, I began to notice occasional disturbing behaviors in my husband—some subtle and some "in your face."

Here are some scenarios that represent PTSD behaviors, both mine and my husband's. The dialogue is between He & Me.

First Scenario – Nightmares & Nightsweats
He: (Snoring, then yelling out!!)
Me: Honey, honey, wake up – you're having a bad dream!
He: Whew. Oh man!! (Shaking)
Me: What were you dreaming about?
He: There was someone chasing me, trying to kill me. I was running scared!!
Me: Well, you must have been running really hard in that dream. Look at you – you're all
sweaty and the sheets are wet. But it's over – go back to sleep. (Now I'm wide awake.)

Same Scenario - Different Night
He: (Screaming out.)
She: Honey wake up—you're having a nightmare!
He: Damn, that was a bad one!

Me: What was it about?

He: I felt like there was someone in our bedroom, a dark shadow coming around the bed to get us!

Me: Well, we're both ok, it was just a bad dream.

He: Yeah, but I'm gonna keep my revolver at the head of our bed from now on.

(This scenario has repeated itself from day one of our marriage even to the present.)

Second Scenario – Antisocial Behavior and Isolation

Me: Honey, how come you just sit all day in front of the computer. Don't you
    want to get out and do something together?

He: Maybe later. (He says moodily).

Me: It concerns me that you don't have any friends or buddies anymore.

He: You're the only friend I need.

Me: Yeah, well you're my best friend too, but I have girlfriends that I go out and have fun with. Don't you miss having friends?

He: No, I don't need any friends. Whenever I've gotten close to buddies they always get killed. It hurts too much to get close to people. And by the way, I don't really like your girlfriend. She is a busy body and I wish you would cool your relationship with her —she's a home-wrecker.

Me: You sound jealous of her.

He: Yes, I am. You spend more time with her than with me.

Me: Maybe it's because lately she's more fun to be with.

(A wall is building between us.)

Third Scenario - Paranoia Will Destroy You

Me: Hey, ya wanna go hiking on the Pacific Crest Trail with me and Leslie today?

He: Yeah, as long as I can pack my pistol.

Me: Do you really think that's necessary? I hike there all the time and never saw a bear or cougar.

He: It's not the bears I'm worried about, it's the people up in them hills. There's a bunch of weirdos up there.

Me: You're the only weirdo—people we meet on the trails should be afraid of you.

He: (Angrily) If you want me to go, I'm taking the damn gun. That's why I have the "concealed weapons" permit!!

Similar Scenario - Suicide

He: Maybe I should do everyone a favor and just kill myself. I don't have much to live for.

Me: Why do you say that? You have so much. You have me and our son and family that love you more than anything. You have a wonderful house and home, money in the bank, a government job with benefits, you've got your health. Why can't you count your blessings?

He: I don't know – I just keep having thoughts about what ifs – what if I just drive my truck off a bridge – everybody would be better off without me.

Me: Please stop thinking like that. Please.

He: I can't – I have no control over these thoughts.

(And the day finally came when he almost did it.)

Fourth Scenario – Anger & Rage

Me: Honey, dinner's ready.

He: Just bring me my dinner, I'm watching a good show on T.V.

Me: Well, me and our son are going to eat at the table and share our day's activities if you want to join in.

He: No thanks.

Me: Y'know, research shows that children fare better in families that share dinner around the table and catch up on everybody's day. Those kids are less likely to get into trouble and drugs and such. The statistics prove it.

He: There's nothing wrong with our boy! Why can't I just eat my dinner and watch T.V. in peace? Why do you have to nag me all the time bitch?!

(He throws the plate of spaghetti at the ceiling. It smashes, leaving the spaghetti hanging from the ceiling)

Me: Well, I'm not cleaning that mess up anymore. You do that all the time!

(I never did clean it up; that spaghetti hung from the ceiling for years until we sold the house.)

These episodes are just the tip of the iceberg of living under the shadow of PTSD. Our home had a steady undercurrent of trauma and drama. It amazes me that I just got used to it – it became normal. For 20 years, I blamed myself. I've tried to figure it all out and fix it; but it was beyond me. It was a different kind of war, a different kind of jungle we lived in. Finally, I said I had to leave and take our son with me, if my husband didn't seek help. We were on the edge of divorce again— about the 5th or 6th time.

Things began to change. He sought help at the VA and actively threw himself into group programs for PTSD and anger management, plus individual counseling. Together we learned about the monster called Post Traumatic Stress Disease, and how it was generating the crazy-making behavior. We learned that PTSD is a progressive disease if you don't get help; that the older you get the worse it affects you if not treated. My husband suffered 30+ years before he got help and I suffered from second hand PTSD for almost as long.

At the VA, he learned tools and techniques for controlling his PTSD and raging anger, and he used them. We also did marriage counseling and 12-step group therapies outside the VA for getting a handle on the addictions that often attach themselves to victims of PTSD. The 12-steps helped me realize I wasn't the cause of my husband's erratic behavior and that it wasn't really me he was angry with. I needed these revelations to begin freeing myself from second hand PTSD.

I thank God for the Veterans Administration. It's no secret that it's a very slow moving government machine, but as frustrating as it is, if you don't give up pounding on their door, they will help you. The VA was an important part of saving our marriage, and probably, our lives. We worked our way through it all and have come out on the other side stronger and wiser than we would be without the hell of this journey. We have found our gold and it is shining brightly.

Today I have my sweet, loving man back – the one I first fell in love with. He's come so far and keeps reclaiming his independence from the prison of PTSD. He's now reaching out to other vets, both older and younger with his music and songs. Today I also have the freedom and energy to reach out to others through the local Hospice Team and through Meals on Wheels. Life is good. This coming October we will celebrate our 30th wedding anniversary!

MOE EATON
WIFE OF ROBERT EATON

I SLEEP NEXT TO PTSD

You read me an article,

The one about your buddy who killed his wife and stuffed her into a foot locker.

This was your relationship disclaimer and I realize it wasn't accidental.

Well, I understand it better now Love,
I sleep next to PTSD.

Hoping that you won't use that Mag light under the bed on me

YOU FREAK MY SHIT OUT, YO!!

You wake us up startled by a noise and jump straight out of bed.

Jesus, it was just the neighbor!

Well, I understand it better now Love,
I sleep next to PTSD.

You call the police to come get your gun.

You ask me to hold you 'cause your tears just won't run.

Well, I understand it better now Love,
I sleep next to PTSD.

You ask me to hide your anxiety pills.

You whisper your plan to take them until your body is still.

Well, I understand it better now Love,
I sleep next to PTSD.

You won't get out of bed, again?

Am I sure that this is who I'll wed?

WELL, I UNDERSTAND BETTER NOW LOVE,
I SLEEP NEXT TO PTSD.

Kat Smith
Friend of Niels Damman

PREVENTIVE MAINTENANCE CHECK AND SERVICES

Nomenclature	human, male
	Operator license # D8890
Body	damaged
Tires	missing in action
Steering wheel	MIA
Gas pedal	inoperable
Horn	inop
Oil	low, no refill available
Spare tire	present but flat, both of them
Fire extinguisher	MIA
Doors	do not fully close
Windshield washer fluid	empty, but would prefer windshield 1st
FA kit	MIA
E brake	inop
All gauges	inop
Mirrors	MIA
Seatbelts	MIA
Lights	inop
Chairs	MIA, although spare tires do suffice
Found a loose part,	origin unknown
Overall state	non mission capable.

REDEPLOY?

NIELS DAMMAN
U.S. ARMY, IRAQ VETERAN

THIS OIF VET IS HEAVILY MEDICATED
FOR YOUR PROTECTION

What you get isn't what you see
If you look closer you'll see a pharmacy
I take the ones that kill the pain
For some odd reason I can't recall its name
Come on now, this one's my friend
Oh yeah, I got it now! It's Vicodin

I swallow down that little tab
It's supposed to keep me from being sad
As it hits my stomach, I feel so soft
You all know it as Zoloft

I look in the mirror before the next one
To remind myself, Jake, this isn't fun
As I read the side effects on the page
It says, "Hey dude! This one's for rage!"

Here's the short, I take it, I'm not as mean.
The docs, they call it…. Clonidine
Scared, twisted, violent…… anxious I am
Times like this I call on…. Lorazepan
You keep me so mellow
You keep me so chill
Your affects are so big, for such a little pill

Explosions, flashes, destructions, and screams
You can't let these in my dreams
Taken before bed and you don't let them in
I wouldn't make it through the night
If it wasn't for my Prazosin

Within 24 hrs I'll take several more
But I won't bore you with them all
I'll just leave you with…. Methocarbomal….
1600 mg's…. man that's not fun
But at least it helps to keep me numb.
If I didn't have these friends I'd cry and moan
Come to think of it
Damn I'm stoned
I've told my story
So I'll take a bow
I hope you all feel safer now.

Dale (Jake) Jacobs
U.S. Air Force, Iraq Veteran

UNTITLED

I was a spectator among the sand
In the heat and the sun
Right near where the Euphrates ran
And I was there as many sides and points of view
Would clash over who could take more away from who
And the brown sand would turn red
And heavy collars would question the men
And others would drown our morale with buckets
of judgment
And time seemed to almost stop as it became
Less of a friend with each passing day
And I was there and watched as an almost
Perpetual loss of life unknown itself
Through our months in the sand
Then I returned home to our country
And as I would look at people in the street
As we passed by each other
None would see the side of me that
Left 22 brothers behind on the other
Side of the world
So those of you in this country whom I'll
Meet, with a handshake, or a kind passing glance
My quiet demeanor may be a suggestion
Or side effect of the loss that I have
experienced.

WILLIAM HALFMOON
U.S. ARMY, IRAQ VETERAN

MY FIRST DATE

She was pretty sitting on the step
(In a preppy college freshman kind of way.)

"Hi," said I.
"Hello," she replied.

"Where are you from," said I.
"Connecticut," she replied.

"I'm from Boston," said I.
"Oh," she replied.

"I'm nervous, I've been out of school," said I.
"Oh?" she replied.

"I was in Vietnam," said I.
"I just got back, I was in the Marines…"

No oh. No nothing.

She quietly rose and walked up the steps.

"I just learned a lesson," said I.
"People here don't care."

There will be no further conversation on this topic.

JACK McLEAN
USMC, VIETNAM VETERAN

A CONVERSATION BETWEEN
MY DAD AND A STRANGER.

Stranger: "Doesn't it bother you that your daughter is 28 and living at home?"

Dad: "If you ever woke up and wondered if your child was still alive, you wouldn't ask me that. I hope she stays forever."

Stranger: "And if she does, then what are you going to do?"

Dad: "Make her breakfast!"

MELISSA STEINMAN
U.S. COAST GUARD, KUWAIT VETERAN

OLD TIMERS – A TERM OF ENDEARMENT

There is no certain path on the road to healing. It is a direction that you take out of a valley surrounded by tall mountains. The underbrush of the forest is thick as a jungle.

From across the valley, a brother runs towards me, and nearly out of breath says, "There was no path to healing when we came back."

"But we are used to cutting through jungles, we started hacking thru the brush 40 years ago, in a direction that might lead to it. We aren't finished yet, we're most of the way up the hill, but we saw you coming, so we ran all the way back to get you. Don't get me wrong, the path is narrow and up hill in all directions, but we have cleared most of the brush before you, and as long as it takes, we will walk it with you."

MELISSA STEINMAN
U.S. COAST GUARD, KUWAIT VETERAN

THAT, WHICH MAKES ME TICK.
TICK, TICK, TICK.

Tick
I sit in the grasses, next to a stream.
I seek comfort here; the world can wait.
Nothing can stop nature
Growth will happen. Life will prevail. The waters will flow.
I drop my filth. It flutters down. All the way down to the ocean.

Birds chirp louder.
Pain washes away.
Nature has done it again.

Tick
I grab my guitar.
6 strings, sound-board I pick a song.
Sorry girl, but I only know 4
Always the same, but sometimes loud, sometimes quietly.
She strums the guitar. She only knows one:
"I'm leaving on a jet plane"
We leave it be and sing.
My heart warms
Music has done it. Again

Tick
My phone vibrates. My niece calls me
 "Niewws"
My dad sends a comic WITH a postcard this time.
We go climbing outside and bring friends along.
My girlfriend comes over and gives me a hug.

I smile, I laugh, I am grateful to be alive.
My friends, my family.
They have done it, yet again

NIELS DAMMAN
U.S. ARMY, IRAQ VETERAN

DON'T MOVE

People might not notice you are here.

Perhaps I won't notice I'm here.

What good does a map do if you don't feel like moving?

NIELS DAMMAN
U.S. ARMY, IRAQ VETERAN

OUR JOURNEY

All I could imagine was your return
but when the time came it would take a turn
I was not prepared for what would come
I thought it would be a time for fun
Instantly I could see that something was missing
for the love of my life I found myself wishing
I can see the emptiness in your eye,
at times it makes me start to cry
I want to help you but I don't know how
I wish I could fix it all right now
I hold it in, it's not about me
for I do not know how you must be
I don't understand how a soldier can be treated this way
There is so much that I have to say
with each day I feel we are healing
As the layers have begun peeling
There are so many times I feel alone
But I thank God each day that you are home.

CHRISTY JACOBS
WIFE OF DALE (JAKE) JACOBS

THE JOURNEY

The journey has been long and difficult

In a sense, you have traveled it alone,

But I was always with you.

The destination injured the souls

that were once joined---

We thought we had it all figured out!

But the souls forgot about the impact

Of their souls on the other

Now it is time to heal these souls

And in doing that......

The two souls will once again

Begin to re-build as one.

CAROLINA HOLNESS
U.S. AIR FORCE, CONUS VETERAN

THE LAST FIELD DRESSING

Above and beyond all things considered, learn to forgive yourself. I don't care what you did or didn't do, try to forgive what you've considered the unforgivable. For there will simply come a day when you finally understand that there is absolutely nothing else left to do. Bring loving people into your life, because you cannot forgive yourself alone. If this was possible, you would have done so a long time ago. Expose emotional silence, so your wounds can finally be healed. It takes time to heal, so give yourself that precious gift. Let the self-inflicted guilt die, instead of you.

MIKE HASTIE
U.S. ARMY MEDIC, VIETNAM VETERAN

SEPARATION, ORDEAL, RETURN

Graduation, Parris Island, and Vietnam
Separated me from my childhood calm
Graduation, Parris Island, and Vietnam.

Parris Island, Vietnam, and all these years
Fueled my ordeal. Stoked my fears.
Parris Island, Vietnam, and all these years.

Meds, Ashland, and Welcome Home
Are framing return to a life of my own.
Thank you meds, Ashland, and Welcome Home.

JACK MCLEAN
USMC, VIETNAM VETERAN

AFTERWORD

HEALING THE WOUNDS OF WAR

Fresh out of graduate school, my first job was with a community-based Vietnam Veterans program. I was hired to counsel veterans struggling with adjustment issues after returning from combat, and to assist with job placement and development. One of my assignments was to help facilitate an on-going "rap" group with the program's therapist. After three weeks of doing the group, the other therapist left the program for another job, leaving me to do the group on my own. With little experience dealing with combat vets other than my conversations with them while I was in the Army and the three sessions that I co-facilitated, I found myself with the daunting task of leading a group for combat veterans.

Having no clinical supervisor or support staff to assist me I immediately began to do a search of the literature for information about doing group therapy—in particular what was appropriate for treating combat veterans. Little did I realize at the time that I was starting a thirty year quest for therapeutic techniques that could be truly effective for treating veterans with combat related issues and adjustment difficulties.

I found numerous books and articles about group psychotherapy, but very little was written about creating therapy groups for combat veterans. Most of the writing at that time described using "rap groups," which were a quasi therapeutic groups aimed at helping Vietnam veterans with their adjustment issues. At that time, adjustment issues and emotional difficulties experienced by Vietnam veterans were titled "delayed stress" or "Post Vietnam Syndrome." About a year and a half later the American Psychiatric Association published a new Diagnostic and Statistical Manual (DSM III). In that manual adjustment problems deriving from battle trauma became known as Post-Traumatic Stress Disorder or PTSD.

By then I was working as a readjustment counseling therapist in a Vet Center, providing group and individual therapy to Vietnam veterans with various levels of PTSD. I had been to several trainings and workshops that focused upon treating the symptoms of PTSD; however it was evident to many of us working in the field that the symptoms listed in DSM III did not explain the full impact of combat on the lives of veterans. It was clear to us that there were more debilitating and enduring effects from exposure to the traumas of war and combat.

For most veterans the sense of self and identity becomes severely disrupted, and their previous views and understandings of society and its common values become challenged during their military experiences. Their very souls had been scarred and wounded, and often their spiritual connection with themselves and the universe had been severely damaged. Treating only the symptoms of PTSD cannot fully repair the larger context and deeper levels of veterans' lives.

My Vet Center peers and I began to discuss the differences between "treatment" and "healing." Beyond addressing critical symptoms interfering with daily functioning, there was clearly a need to work with the veterans on deeper levels of healing from their war wounds. Genuine healing happens when a veteran becomes able to incorporate the skills and knowledge learned from treating their symptoms in ways that allow them to rebuild relationships with self, family, and community. Healing means that veterans regain a sense of belonging and purpose in their lives, find meaningful work, and establish conscious and healthy connections to their families and communities.

As my work and training progressed I became more skilled at treating the symptoms of PTSD in both individual and group therapy settings. I acquired new and helpful techniques for addressing PTSD symptoms, such as emotional constriction, intrusive thoughts, recurring memories, and nightmares. As I deepened my understanding of the disorder, I also began to see the need for broader strategies to focus on psychosocial aspects of care for the wounded warrior. At the Vet Center we began to offer couples counseling and support groups for the veterans and their partners as a way of assisting the veterans to develop more healthy relationships and stable support systems. We began to offer more training to assist the veterans with communication skills, anger management, employment assistance, supportive services for employment and job retention skills. To help veterans reconnect with the community we organized groups to march in Veterans Day parades. For their wounded souls, we brought in priests and ministers, as well as native healers, to work with the warriors on healing the spirit.

As another example, in 1983 we helped to organize a group trip to the dedication of the Vietnam Veteran Memorial in Washington DC. After returning, several veterans helped to organize and implement a Vietnam Veterans Memorial in Oregon. We supported and assisted this effort, seeing it as a vehicle for helping connect the veterans to the community and giving them a sense of purpose and meaning. While not directly related to the symptoms of PTSD, the effort, energy, and talents that the veterans utilized in bringing the memorial to fruition became an integral part of healing their wounds from war. Over the years I continued to look for opportunities to assist the veterans and encouraged their participation in sporting events, veterans' organizations, volunteer activities, and community events. As a therapist with extensive experience assisting veterans to heal their war wounds I knew that simply treating the symptoms of PTSD would never be enough; that it is necessary to address the effects of battle traumas on many levels of their lives.

When I first heard about the Welcome Home project my initial thought was: "Here is another well-intentioned project that may not get off the ground and could wind up doing harm to the veterans." Over thirty years of experience I had seen many projects begin brightly only to fail to fully materialize when the going got rough. Some projects intensified the traumas and isolation of veterans because they were unable to engage the necessary community support, could not attract enough veterans to continue, or simply failed to learn how to work with vets. However, I was intrigued enough to look further into what was being proposed in case it might work. If it was well planned and fully carried out, it might offer both veterans and civilian communities a much needed vehicle for genuine healing.

I met with the Bill McMillan, one of the organizers of the event, to see if he knew what he was getting into. I became convinced that not only would the Welcome Home Project happen, but that it had the potential to succeed, to offer veterans an opportunity to heal some of the inner wounds, and to create a meaningful dialogue with community members. Some thirty years ago I read an article by Robert Bly that stated that healing from the Vietnam War could not happen without the American public being able to grieve the wounds and losses that had taken place and acknowledge the role the public had played in the war. The Welcome Home Project seemed to offer an opportunity for both the veterans and the community to do just that. I agreed to work with Bill and signed on as a therapist and as support staff for the program. What convinced me to work with the program was that Michael Meade would be facilitating the retreat. I had read some of Michael's work, seen a tape of one of his retreats, and knew that he was skilled enough to make this project therapeutic and healing for both participating veterans and family members.

During the retreat I felt honored to be part of the program and inspired by the opportunity to work with some outstanding veterans and staff. We came to the retreat from different wars and various branches of the service. It took a few days to get to know each other and move past our surface differences, but thanks to the skill of Michael and his staff we were soon working as a coherent group united in our effort to heal the wounds of war. I was impressed by how hard everyone involved worked. I had never before seen a group of strangers become open and flexible enough to move past the usual issues and differences and form a cohesive unit in such a short period of time.

The veterans were courageous and generous with their thoughts and feelings as they spoke out and worked extremely hard on their writings. They committed their hearts and their souls to the words they put on paper. They were able to see how their deep revelations and poetic words were not just a personal process, but also a direct contribution in helping to heal each other. It was an amazing process to be a part of and involved some of the most impressive and impacting healing that I have seen in my many years as a therapist. I would encourage all trauma therapists to look beyond the treatment of PTSD symptoms and expand their work to engage veterans in the kind of creative and truly healing practices that we experienced during the retreat and the Voices of Veterans presentation.

MICHAEL J. MAXWELL, MS

ACKNOWLEDGEMENTS

Veterans, Family Members, and Friends

To those who accepted the risk of opening their hearts and sharing their experiences of war, we owe the greatest gratitude. Without their courage, none of this would have been possible.

Laura Carpenter, Eli Painted Crow, Niels Damman, Rory Dunn, Bob Eaton, Moe Eaton, Deborah Guerrero, William Halfmoon, Mike Hastie, Carolina Holness, Joseph Holness, Dale (Jake) Jacobs, Christy Jacobs, Ken Kraft, Cynthia LeFever, Stan LeFever, Mandy Martin, Jack McClean, Dan Nielsen, Mike Schenk, Dan Shea, Kat Smith, Melissa Steinman.

Faculty, Support Staff, and Film Crew

We offer special appreciation to the staff and film crew who worked endlessly and contributed unparalleled expertise to make the events an artful reality.

Andrew Black, Bob Kimball, Leigh Kimball, Jacob Lakatua, Michael Maxwell, Lauren McLagen, Bill McMillan, Henry McMillan, Michael Meade, Lauretta Molitor, Carl Robinson, Peggy Rubin, Kim Shelton.

The Welcome Home Project and Mosaic Multicultural Foundation wish to thank the individuals, organizations, and businesses in Ashland and throughout Southern Oregon, too numerous to name, for their generous support, and donations of funds, time and services. Special thanks go to the Oregon Shakespeare Festival, the staff at Buckhorn Springs Retreat Center, and the Grants Pass Vet Center, the Portland Vet Center and the Southern Oregon, White City Rehabilitation Center.

We are deeply grateful to all who contributed, supported, and welcomed our deserving veterans.

ABOUT THE WELCOME HOME PROJECT

The Welcome Home Project was created in collaboration with Michael Meade and the **Mosaic Multicultural Foundation** to provide a healing retreat for veterans and family members from wars in Vietnam, Iraq, and Afghanistan. Just as important, our goal was to bring the veterans and the civilian public together in a large welcome home ceremony that is crucial for both the veterans and the communities to which they return. Without this welcome, many veterans live in isolation with a deep sense of betrayal, while civilians carry on in numbness and denial of the realities of war and its effects on the men and women who serve, and upon their families and communities as well.

These poems were created by the veterans of the Welcome Home Project Retreat and were presented to an appreciative and grateful public on Memorial Day, 2008. People still stop us on the street to express their gratitude for the event and for the men and women who had the courage to step forth on the stage to speak the truth.

The primary focus of *The Welcome Home Project* at this point is to produce a feature length documentary which will be edited over the course of the next year. This is a film of both the veterans retreat and the Voices of Veterans ceremony at the Bowmer Theater in Ashland on Memorial Day, 2008.

For questions or for more information contact Kim Shelton, film director, at 541-482-7090, or email at: shelton@ccountry.net. Other information on the Welcome Home Project can be found at www.thewelcomehomeproject.org.

ABOUT MOSAIC

Mosaic Multicultural Foundation is a 501(c)3 nonprofit organization, a network of artists, social activists, and community builders. Mosaic formed to create cross-cultural alliances, mentoring relationships, and social connections that encourage greater understanding between diverse peoples, elders and youth, veterans and civilians, and those with various cultural and spiritual backgrounds.

Mosaic means putting essential pieces together; forming a whole from separate, divided, even estranged parts. The process of finding, fitting and weaving together divergent, yet necessary pieces involves making new social fabrics from existing ethnic, spiritual, psychological and political threads.

Mosaic events draw inspiration from the traditions of many cultures and incorporate knowledge learned in the trenches of contemporary community work. Efforts at problem solving rely on locating the genius of the situation, as the unique spirit of each individual becomes a key to understanding issues and fitting the pieces of community together in new ways.

GreenFire Press and **Mosaic Audio** are imprints of Mosaic Multicultural Foundation that serve to foster cultural literacy, mythic education, and multicultural community development. Proceeds from sales of books and recordings directly benefit Mosaic's work with at-risk youth, refugees, veterans, and intercultural projects.

For more information contact Mosaic:
4218 1/2 SW Alaska, Suite H Seattle, WA 98126
(206)935-3665, toll free (800)233-6984
www.mosaicvoices.org ~ info@mosaicvoices.org